D0344143

565-1

OIL SPILLS

© Aladdin Books Ltd 2003

Designed and produced by
Aladdin Books Ltd
28 Percy Street
London W1T 2BZ

Revised and updated edition published in 2003
First published in Great Britain in 1993 by
Franklin Watts
96 Leonard Street
London EC2A 4XD

ISBN: 0 7496 4953 4

Design: David West Children's Book Design
Designer: Stephen Woosnam-Savage
Editors: Fiona Robertson
               Brian Hunter Smart
               Jim Pipe
Picture research: Emma Krikler
               Brian Hunter Smart
Illustrator: Mike Saunders

A catalogue record for this book is available from the
British Library.

Printed in UAE
All rights reserved

Environmental Disasters

OIL SPILLS

JANE WALKER

FRANKLIN WATTS
LONDON • SYDNEY

CONTENTS

INTRODUCTION

Recent pictures of dramatic oil spills show helpless birds struggling to escape from an oil-coated sea, or treacle-like waves of jet black oil washing onto sandy beaches and rocky shores. These are just some of the consequences of a major spill of crude oil at sea.

Each year, several million tonnes of used oil end up on our land and in our seas and rivers. While some of this oil is spilled by accident, a far greater number of oil spills are the result of human actions.

Strict controls are needed to reduce the devastating damage that is caused. In the end, the world may need to turn to cleaner and safer forms of energy to avoid many of the disastrous effects caused by oil spills.

AN OILY MESS

All the world's oceans and seas are polluted with oil. Each day, the world uses over 12,000 million litres of oil. Most of this oil is transported around the world in huge tankers. Accidental spills or leakages, as well as deliberate dumping, have left the world's busiest shipping routes severely affected by oil pollution.

When oil is spilled at sea, either deliberately or accidentally, it covers a huge patch of sea, forming a giant oil slick. High winds or rough seas can push the slick onto nearby shores, covering rocks and sandy beaches in thick black oil, and causing serious harm to wildlife.

Oil forms a thick greasy layer on the water's surface. This oily film blocks out vital supplies of light and air to marine life in the water below. Some of the oil evaporates but most of it forms into balls of tar that drift along on the water's surface. Eventually the spilled oil breaks down and disperses, but by this time it has caused widespread damage.

→ When as little as 1 litre of oil is spilled onto water, it rapidly covers an area that is equal in size to half a football pitch. Imagine the area of sea that is covered with oil when a fully-loaded tanker runs aground and spills millions of litres of oil.

6

↑ In August 1983, the *Castillo de Bellver* tanker (above) ruptured in two off the coast of Cape Town and spilled over 320 million litres of oil. Wildlife along the South African coast was again threatened by a large oil slick when the *Jolly Rubino* ran aground in January 2002.

→ Crude oil is the black sticky substance which is drilled out from reservoirs trapped in the rocks underground or under the seabed. At an oil refinery, the crude oil is changed into products such as petroleum and diesel oil.

HOW DO OIL SPILLS OCCUR?

Thousands of millions of litres of oil spill into the ocean each year, but the big oil spills that you hear about on the news account for just 5 per cent of all spills. Much of the oil polluting the ocean comes from small spills on land. The principal source of this pollution is used engine oil, often carelessly poured away down drains and onto waste land.

Another common source of oil spills is from ships discharging waste engine oil into the sea. Oil tankers also add oil to the sea while cleaning their cargo tanks.

Though tanker accidents have caused most of the biggest oil spills, the largest accidental oil spill in history occurred in June 1979 when the *IXTOC I* oil well blew out off the east coast of Mexico. By the time the well was brought under control, 500 million litres of oil had been spilled.

Oil spills can also be the result of deliberate human actions. In January 1991, retreating Iraqi troops set oil wells on fire and ruptured pipelines in Kuwait at the northern end of the Persian Gulf (p.18), causing perhaps the biggest oil spill ever.

Many spills result from accidents involving pipelines or fixed facilities. Oil enters the sea from oil terminals and refineries situated along the coastline. Routine maintenance contributes 620 million litres of oil to our inshore seas, whilst offshore drilling adds 65 million litres due to operational discharges (p.11) and accidental spills.

Some ocean oil "pollution" is natural. Seepage from the ocean bottom and eroding sedimentary rocks releases another 280 million litres.

← An underground explosion or a fire on board a drilling platform (left) can cause large quantities of oil to leak into the sea.

Spills and leakages from oil refineries

↑ In June 1990, an explosion on board the *Mega Borg*, a Norwegian supertanker, resulted in over 23 million litres of crude oil spilling into the Gulf of Mexico. Rough seas often break up a damaged tanker before its oil cargo can be offloaded.

Oil tanker accidents

Discharges from ships and tankers at sea

Leakages from oil pipelines are a major source of spills

Leakages and waste dumped from oil drilling platforms

THE DAMAGE

Oil spills at sea are often carried long distances by ocean currents, tides and strong winds. A major spill from a tanker at sea can pollute many thousands of kilometres of coastline.

Oil spills are responsible for the destruction of entire wildlife habitats, and for killing or injuring large sea creatures such as whales and seals, as well as seabirds, fish and small seashore animals such as barnacles and snails. Plankton, the tiny plants and animals which live on and below the water's surface, also die from oil pollution.

Plankton form the basis of many marine food chains as well as being the food source that supports larger marine creatures such as whales.

Along the shoreline, the spilled oil mixes with sand and eventually sinks down onto the sea-bed. Here it destroys the feeding and breeding grounds of creatures such as oysters and mussels.

Oil coats beaches and rocky shores, ruining beauty spots and popular tourist resorts. Local people who depend on tourism or fishing have their livelihoods threatened by this pollution.

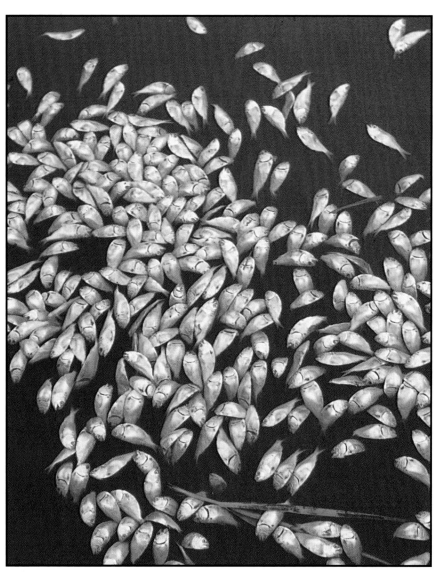

← Fish die in oil-polluted waters because of a shortage of oxygen in the water. The oil also coats their eggs and larvae, causing the young fish to be born damaged.

↓ A fire broke out on board the *Piper Alpha* oil platform (below) in the North Sea in 1988, killing 167 workers. Around 1.8 million litres of oil were spilled.

Drilling equipment

The drill bit cuts through hard rock in search of oil below the sea-bed. Oil-based muds are pumped down the drill shaft during drilling operations.

Oil companies use oil-based "muds" when drilling for oil under the sea-bed. The muds lubricate the drill bits and help to stop oil escaping from the drilling shaft. About 10 per cent of this mud consists of oil. Some of the oil is removed before the used muds are dumped into the sea, but around three-quarters of the oil pollution from the offshore oil industry comes from this source.

Derrick

A metal structure, called a derrick, stands on the oil platform. The derrick is used to lower and raise the drilling equipment.

Oil production platform

This is a semi-submersible oil platform. Its legs are flooded with water to hold the platform down on the sea-bed.

Oil discharges

Oil platforms also discharge "produced" water into the sea. This water is left behind when the oil is removed from the water and oil mixture that is pumped out of the sea-bed.

WILDLIFE IN DANGER

Thousand of animals die in the world's oil-polluted waters each year. Oil quickly spreads out across water, creating a greasy film over the surface. It sticks to the bodies of sea-birds such as grebes and cormorants, clogging their feathers. The birds become unable to fly and, because the oil affects their buoyancy, they cannot float either. As the feathers become coated with oil, they no longer insulate the bird's body against the cold.

In December 2002, the *Prestige* tanker sank off the coast of northern Spain. The pressure of the water three kilometres deep caused the already badly corroded tanks to split, and its cargo of 60 million litres of heavy fuel oil began to slowly leak out. Within a week, 10,000 birds had been killed by the oil, which also polluted nearby breeding grounds for many species of shark, dolphin, seal and turtle.

Marine mammals, such as seals and sea otters, swallow oil from the water or from their fur as they try to clean it off their bodies. Other creatures starve to death when their food supply, which consists of plankton, is poisoned. The oil also causes serious damage to sea-water habitats such as seagrass meadows and coral reefs.

← During bad weather, sea-birds may mistake an area of oily water for calm sea. Sea-birds caught in an oil slick die either from drowning, exposure to the cold or from poisoning as they try to clean the oil from their feathers during preening. Those that are rescued may be taken to a special centre, where they are fed a mixture of water, sugar and salt. They are then cleaned with detergent.

↑ Oil from the tanker *San Jorge* polluted the shores and coastline of Uruguay in February 1997. The rocks and sandy beaches of this shoreline were heavily polluted. The sea-lion pup in this photo was covered in oil as were many others along the coast as this is a breeding and nursery area for sea-lions. Over 200 pups were killed by the spill.

The Baltic Sea

The Baltic Sea is one of the world's most ecologically fragile stretches of water. This semi-enclosed sea has almost no tides or tidal currents, so the rate of water renewal here is very slow. The lack of new water means that pollutants are not easily dispersed.

The seawater here is very cold and not very salty. This makes the Baltic Sea a unique environment — many of the animals living here cannot live anywhere else.

Heavy industrialization of the Baltic States has also contributed to the massive environmental degradation of the Baltic Sea.

Oil pollution also threatens the local fishing industry, below, which is important to the economies of the Baltic countries.

THE *EXXON VALDEZ*

Oil spills have to be dealt with quickly. In March 1989, in calm seas, the *Exxon Valdez* supertanker ran aground in Prince William Sound in Alaska, USA. Within 24 hours of the accident, over 45 million litres of crude oil had spilled into the sea from the damaged tanker. A further 182 million litres of oil were still on board the tanker.

Some 12 hours after the accident, the emergency services had still not arrived to deal with the disaster. Within two days, an oil slick covered over 75 square kilometres. The clean-up operation was not only slow to start, but also ineffective. Only 1 per cent of the oil spill had been recovered 72 hours after the accident.

Before the disaster, the area around Prince William Sound was one of unspoiled beauty. It has major ecological importance, with several national wildlife refuges and national parks being located nearby. Due to the failure to contain the oil spill immediately after the accident, over **4,000 kilometres** of Alaskan coastline were polluted.

Stormy weather and high winds moved the slick a distance of over 60 kilometres overnight. The oil was carried onto nearby shores. Millions of fish died as a result of this disaster, as well as more than 300,000 sea-birds. Bald eagles, which were already an endangered species, also became victims of the oil spill, as the oil poisoned their food supply.

← Recovery and response vessels eventually reached the supertanker *Exxon Valdez* (left). Containment booms were also deployed but by then the damage had been done. The slow response to the spill was a major factor in the scale of this ecological disaster.

→ The clean-up operation (right) used high-pressure hot water hoses and vacuum pumps.

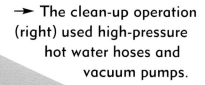

Prince William Sound

Exxon Valdez

Oil slick

GULF OF ALASKA

← Eleven days after the *Exxon Valdez* had first run aground, its remaining oil cargo was removed to a second tanker. The damaged supertanker was then pulled off the rocks. Its wrecked hull was taken to San Diego, USA, for examination (shown left). At the time of the accident, the tanker was off course and outside the official shipping lanes.

OIL FROM THE LAND

Each year, human beings dispose of more than 5,000 million litres of used oil on land. The oil seeps into the ground, contaminating underground water sources and polluting our supplies of drinking water.

The seas around very densely populated cities, where there are large numbers of cars and vehicles, are often the worst affected. Every year the oily road runoff from a city of 5 million people could contain as much oil as one large tanker spill. The Mediterranean is surrounded by major cities and towns, consequently it is heavily polluted with oil. There are virtually no tides in the Mediterranean, so the oil cannot easily be washed away, broken up or dispersed.

Oil can leak onto the land from faulty pipelines or storage tanks. In 1984, a crack in a pipeline at a Brazilian oil refinery near the city of São Paulo led to the deaths of over 500 people. Thousands of litres of oil spilled out onto the surface of a nearby swamp. The oil caught fire and destroyed 2,500 homes in the shanty town of Vila Socco.

⯆ Land-based drilling operations are another source of oil pollution. "Nodding donkeys", such as the ones shown below in California, are one of the commonest ways of drilling for oil on land.

→ The photo on the right shows a burning pool of crude oil from the Sacha oil field in the Amazonian rainforest of Ecuador. Foreign oil companies have taken over a large proportion of the rainforest in this area. Pools of oil such as the one shown here can be found beside each well. Oil is dumped into the pool every six months when the well is cleaned. This pool has been set on fire accidentally by colonists burning a nearby section of rainforest.

↓ On land, oil forms an invisible film over the soil, acting as a seal that prevents water and oxygen from penetrating below the surface. In this way, it harms creatures such as earthworms, which play a vital role in keeping the soil healthy and fertile. The oil also ends up in rivers, such as the one below, where it reduces the oxygen supply that fish and other aquatic animals depend on for survival.

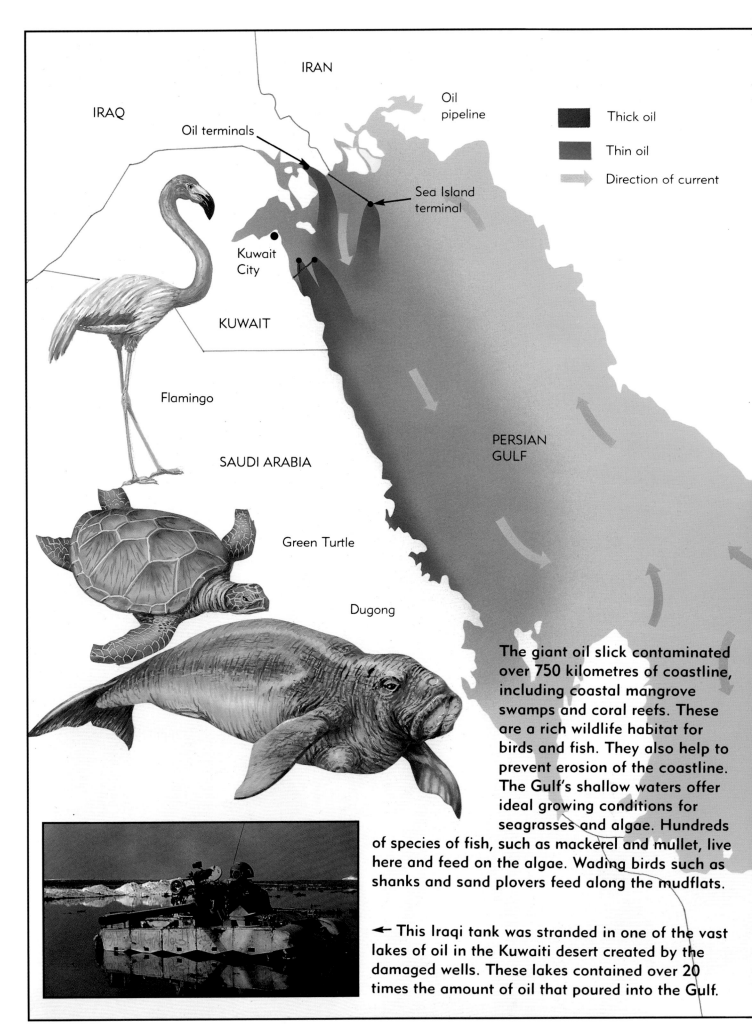

IRAN

IRAQ

Oil pipeline

Oil terminals

Sea Island terminal

	Thick oil
	Thin oil
→	Direction of current

Kuwait City

KUWAIT

Flamingo

SAUDI ARABIA

PERSIAN GULF

Green Turtle

Dugong

The giant oil slick contaminated over 750 kilometres of coastline, including coastal mangrove swamps and coral reefs. These are a rich wildlife habitat for birds and fish. They also help to prevent erosion of the coastline. The Gulf's shallow waters offer ideal growing conditions for seagrasses and algae. Hundreds of species of fish, such as mackerel and mullet, live here and feed on the algae. Wading birds such as shanks and sand plovers feed along the mudflats.

← This Iraqi tank was stranded in one of the vast lakes of oil in the Kuwaiti desert created by the damaged wells. These lakes contained over 20 times the amount of oil that poured into the Gulf.

THE PERSIAN GULF

The Persian Gulf is one of the world's busiest sea-lanes for oil tanker traffic. The countries which border onto the Gulf — Iran, Iraq, Kuwait, Saudi Arabia, Bahrain and the United Arab Emirates — are all major oil producers. Each year, the equivalent of almost 300 million litres of oil spills or leaks into its shallow waters, making the Gulf the most polluted body of water in the world.

Yet an even greater source of pollution threatened this area in 1991, at the end of the Gulf War. The departing Iraqi soldiers set fire to more than 600 Kuwaiti oil wells, which burned for several months. Oil refineries and other installations were also seriously damaged. The resulting oil slick was the biggest ever and threatened the ecosystem of the whole Persian Gulf.

Valuable fishing grounds are found in the Gulf, where shrimps, oysters and prawns are farmed. Also at risk were dugongs, or sea cows, which were already threatened with extinction. Dolphins and green turtles were affected, as well as the endangered hawksbill turtle, which lays its eggs on the local islands. The oil slick also claimed the lives of more than 20,000 birds.

An estimated 1 billion litres or more of crude oil poured out from the damaged Kuwaiti oil wells (right). Vast lakes of oil were created, some measuring up to 1.5 kilometres long and 1 metre deep. The spilled oil threatened to pollute the water supply of Kuwait City. It also released poisonous gases into the air, and harmed wildlife habitats by contaminating soil and local vegetation.

DISASTER AT SEA

In March 1967, an oil tanker called the *Torrey Canyon* ran aground off the coast of Cornwall, between Land's End and the Scilly Isles. Millions of litres of crude oil were released into the sea, forming an oil slick almost 30 kilometres long.

At the time, this was the biggest pollution problem that had ever threatened the British coastline.

By the end of March, the slick from the *Torrey Canyon* covered an area of **650 square kilometres. During attempts to salvage the damaged tanker, it began to break up, pouring more oil into the sea. Planes sprayed the tanker with fuel and then bombed it in order to burn off the remaining oil cargo. Large amounts of detergents were also sprayed onto the oil slick.**

Some 11 years later, the world's worst oil tanker spill occured on the other side of the English Channel. The *Amoco Cadiz* tanker ran onto the rocks off the coast of Brittany in northern France in March 1978, spilling 260 million litres of crude oil.

The resulting oil slick polluted over 150 kilometres of French beaches. It caused extensive damage to the local fishing industry, ruining oyster beds and lobster fishing grounds.

Oil-covered beaches

Mixture of thick and thin oil

Torrey Canyon

Land's End

Truro

CORNWALL

Falmouth

Thin oil

Thick oil

← The *Amoco Cadiz* was not in a seaworthy condition at the time of the accident. The tanker had been pushed onto the rocks when its steering equipment failed. At one stage, it seemed as if the slick might reach the Channel Islands, the Scilly Isles and the Cornish coast.

Ocean traffic

Oil spills happen more frequently in certain parts of the world. The following waters are "hot spots" for oil spills from vessels: the Gulf of Mexico, the northeastern USA, the Mediterranean Sea, the Persian Gulf, the North Sea, the Sea of Japan and the Baltic Sea. The map above shows the world's principal oil tanker routes (marked in red). Accidents often occur in busy shipping lanes, such as in the English Channel and the North Sea.

↓ In August 1993, three ships collided in Tampa Bay, off the US coast: the barge *Bouchard B115*, the freighter *Balsa 37* and the barge *Ocean 255*. The *Bouchard B115* spilled an estimated 1.5 million litres of fuel oil into Tampa Bay. Below is a photo of the *Ocean 255* after the collision.

OPERATION CLEAN-UP

It is vital that rescue services take action within the first few hours after an oil spill at sea. Different methods and tools are used, depending on the weather, the type and amount of oil spilled, how near to shore the oil spill is and the local habitat.

Large booms stop the spread of oil while skimming vessels remove oil floating on the water's surface. Big sponges are also used to soak up the oil. Some spills are sprayed with chemicals to break them up.

Oil can also be burned off the sea, but this method produces a thick black smoke that can harm people and wildlife living nearby. In areas where the water and air temperatures are high, some of the oil evaporates naturally off the sea.

On land, oil has to be removed from the sand and rocks along the shore. Spreading fertiliser along the beaches causes the growth of tiny organisms which break down the oil and clean it up.

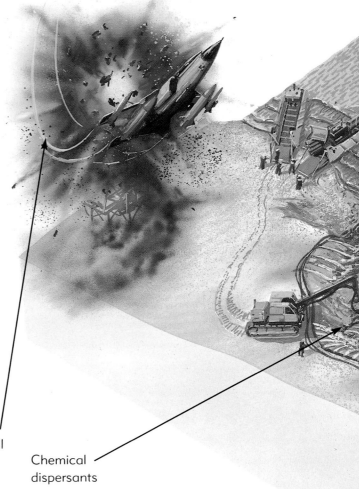

↑ To clean up an oil slick at sea, chemicals are sprayed onto the oil, either from a ship (shown above) or from an aeroplane. The chemicals help to disperse the slick by separating the droplets of oil. However, the effects of some chemicals may be poisonous to fish and other forms of marine life.

Explosive dropped on damaged oil well or tanker

Chemical dispersants

When the *Prestige* sank off Spain in November 2002, eight ships sucked around 6 million litres of oil from it before it sank. The mini-submarine *Nautile* was also used to examine the wreck on the seabed.

➤ Large floating barriers, called booms (right), prevent oil from spreading on the surface of the water. The booms are transported to the spill area and then attached to the back of tugboats or other small craft. If necessary, the slick can then be redirected to another area.

Damaged oil tanker

Skimming vessel

Oil slick

Boom

High-pressure water hoses

If oil is quickly restricted to a small area of the sea, and the damaged ship is repaired or its oil cargo off-loaded, the pollution threat from the spill is greatly reduced.

WHAT CAN WE DO?

The more people rely on oil the greater the risk there is of oil spills. So all of us share the responsibility for finding ways to solve the problem.

If we avoid dumping oil into the sewer or rubbish bin, we avoid polluting the environment we live in. Also, when we use less oil, less needs to be transported, and there's a lower risk of future spills. For example, we can walk or take the bus rather than taking a car on short journeys.

Oil companies must do more to prevent spills. Accidental spills can be reduced by limiting the actual size of cargo tanks. Oil companies should also discharge the waste from oil-based drilling muds at properly-equipped facilities. Oil-based muds could be replaced by water-based muds at only a slightly higher cost. At sea, the dumping of oil and washing-out of cargo tanks must be even more tightly controlled. Scientists can now trace an oil spill back to the tanker that discharged it.

Recycling centres need to be set up to collect the used oil from car engines (above). They are particularly needed in city areas where there are large numbers of vehicles.

The waste oil can be recycled into lubricating or heating oil. Improved port facilities are needed for tankers and other ships, so that unwanted oil can be disposed of safely.

↑ Regular checks need to be made of any oil-carrying equipment, such as storage tanks and pipelines.

The giant Alaska pipeline (above) carries oil from the oilfields of the frozen north to terminals such as Valdez on the Alaskan coast. The pipeline has corroded in places, and more than US$1,000 million worth of repair work is needed.

← Factories, refineries and other oil installations, such as these crude oil storage tanks in Texas, USA, must be prevented from leaking oil onto land or into the sea.

Heavy fines can be introduced to deter oil companies from allowing such leakages. Oil companies must also be forced to meet the cost of cleaning up spillages.

PROTECTING OUR SEAS

Worldwide shipping is regulated by the International Maritime Organization (IMO)'s convention on ship-generated pollution. This was first proposed in 1973, then extended in 1978, and is known as MARPOL 73/78. By May 2002, over 95 per cent of the world's shipping was subject to its regulations. Between 1981 and 1989, MARPOL was largely responsible for a 60 per cent reduction in the amount of oil pollution released from ships. It should have an even greater effect in coming years as many of the giant supertankers built in the 1970s will be scrapped as it will be too expensive to bring them up to the standards of the MARPOL convention.

Constant monitoring of pollution levels at sea is an important aspect of protecting against oil spills. In the past, this has been done by ships or planes, but satellites are now being used to detect oil slicks from space using the Synthetic Aperture Radar. This can pick up oil slicks in all weathers and at any time of day or night.

The coastlines of countries which have ratified MARPOL 73/78 by 2002

MARPOL 73/78 bans oil discharges within 93 kilometres (50 nautical miles) of any coastline. The MARPOL Convention introduced a better method of cleaning cargo tanks, called crude oil washing.

In the past, empty tanks were washed out with sea-water, which left behind a mixture of oil and water that was difficult to get rid of. Now, tankers use part of their crude oil cargo to remove the sediments inside their tanks.

↑ The workers shown above are removing oil spilled from a tanker off the town of Huntington Beach in California. The Oil Pollution Act of 1990 established a fund to clean up oil spills throughout the United States, and set regulations for storage facilities and transport vessels. Individual states, such as California, also have their own comprehensive offshore oil spill prevention plans.

→ More than 50,000 commercial ships are in operation on the world's seas today, including around 3,000 oil tankers. Regular checks on pollution levels help to ensure that our seas remain clean.

THE FUTURE

The most effective way to win the fight against oil pollution is to reduce our consumption of oil. Each day, the world uses over 12 billion litres of oil. By using alternative sources of energy, such as wind power and solar power, we can lessen the pollution risk. Governments around the world also need to examine the risks of new proposals to extract oil.

The problem of oil spills on land will be helped by creating more recycling facilities. Improved reception facilities in ports will help to reduce oil discharges at sea. Technology can lead to the design of safer and cleaner tankers. In 1991, the US government announced that all tankers sailing within 320 kilometres of the US coastline must be equipped with a double hull by the year 2015.

All ships built after 1996 must have double hulls, but there are still many older, single-hulled tankers in use. The oil spill caused by the ageing *Prestige* in December 2002 highlighted this problem and prompted the European Union to propose a ban on single-hull tankers and set about establishing a European Maritime Safety Agency.

Ballast tanks

Oil tanks

Double hull

Designs for safer oil tankers include additional protection for the oil-carrying tanks and special safety features to prevent the escape of oil after an accident.

A Japanese design, called the mid-deck tanker, has special wing ballast tanks. These provide additional protection following a collision. In a double-hull tanker, the cargo tanks are separated from the ship's outer hull to protect against the impact of an accident.

Protected fuel tanks

Satellite equipment helps rescue services to locate tanker

Pumps to transfer oil in an emergency

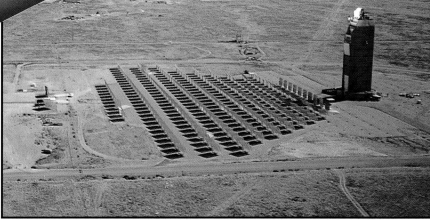

← An alternative fuel to petrol is gasohol, which is made out of the alcohol obtained from sugars found in crops such as maize. By developing such alternative fuels, the world can reduce its oil consumption.

↑ At present, solar power provides less than 1 per cent of the world's energy needs. Although the equipment needed for solar energy is expensve, the energy from the Sun itself is free, limitless and relatively clean.

FACT FILE

Crude oil measures
1 tonne = 7.5 barrels
1 barrel = 159 litres

Exxon Valdes
To date, the clean-up operation after this disaster has cost more than US $2,500 billion. Although the state of Alaska in the United States contains huge reserves of oil, many new drilling proposals have been blocked following this catastrophic oil spill.

Persian Gulf
During the clean-up operation after the Gulf War, oil-skimming ships recovered between 20,000 and 30,000 barrels of oil a day. The Saudi Arabian oil company Saudi Aramco laid around 40 kilometres of boom and sent a fleet of more than 20 oil-recovery craft to the disaster site.

Recent oil spills
1989
March — the tanker *Exxon Valdez* hit an undersea reef in Prince William Sound off the coast of Alaska, spilling over 45 million litres of oil into the sea, the worst oil spill in US history.

December — an explosion on an Iranian supertanker, the *Kharg-5*, 720 kilometres north of Las Palmas, caused over 85 million litres of crude oil to spill into Atlantic Ocean. This created a 30 square-kilometre oil slick that threatened the coast of Morocco in North Africa.

1990
June — as a result of an explosion and fire, the tanker *Mega Borg* released 23 million litres of oil into the Gulf of Mexico near Galveston, Texas.

1991
January — during the Gulf War, Iraqi soldiers released an estimated 1 billion or more litres of crude oil into the Persian Gulf by damaging Kuwaiti oil wells.

1992
December — the Greek tanker, *Aegean Sea*, split in two after an accident off the north-west coast of Spain. The oil from its almost 100 million-litre cargo threatened the local fishing and shellfish industries.

1994
September — a dam, built to contain oil, burst and spilled oil into a tributary of the Kolva River in Russia. The spill may have been as large as 300 million litres.

1996
February — the supertanker *Sea Empress* ran aground near the port of Milford Haven, Wales, spewing out 78 million litres of crude oil in a 40-kilometre slick.

1999
December — the tanker *Erika* broke apart and sank off Brittany, France, spilling 13.5 million litres of oil into the sea.

2000
January — a burst pipeline owned by the Brazilian government-owned oil company, Petrobras, spilt 1.5 million litres of heavy oil into Guanabara Bay near Rio de Janeiro, Brazil.

November — the oil tanker *Westchester* ran aground south of New Orleans, USA, dumping 2.5 million litres of crude oil into the Mississippi River.

2001
January — the tanker *Jessica* ran aground off the Galapagos' San Cristobal Island, leaking about 910,000 litres of fuel. Luckily, favourable winds and sea currents helped push most of the oil into the open sea, narrowly averting a full-scale environmental disaster. However, scientists blamed the spill for the deaths of 15,000 marine iguanas on the island of Santa Fe.

2002
December — the tanker *Prestige* was carrying more than 90 million litres of oil when it was damaged in a fierce storm 45 kilometres off the coast of Spain. Almost immediately, 6 million litres of oil leaked into the ocean and washed ashore along the Spanish coastline. After it sank, oil continued to leak from its hull, polluting northern Spanish and southwestern French coastlines.

GLOSSARY

algae – a group of plants that grow in fresh and salt water. Some algae are microscopic, others grow much bigger, such as seaweed.

bacteria – tiny living things that can help to break down dead plant and animal material and other substances.

ballast – heavy material, such as water or lumps of metal, which is placed inside a ship to make it stable.

boom – a floating barrier which is made of plastic or rubber and stops the spread of oil on water.

corrode – to wear away slowly.

crude oil – a black sticky substance found beneath the ground and the sea-bed. Petroleum and other fuels are made from crude oil.

derrick – a metal, tower-like structure found on an oil drilling rig. It is placed over the drilling shaft.

detergent – a chemical substance that helps droplets of oil to spread out in water.

discharge – to pour out.

disperse – to make a substance break up and spread out.

drilling mud – a mixture of oil and water which is used when drilling for oil.

ecosystem – a community of living things and their natural surroundings.

evaporate – to change from a liquid to a gas or vapour.

extract – to remove from under the Earth's surface.

gasohol – a fuel that is made from the sugars found in crops such as sugar cane and maize.

insulate – to prevent the escape of heat.

lubricate – to add oil or grease to a machine to make it work smoothly.

oil-based mud – see drilling mud.

oil slick – a smooth area of water that is covered with oil.

plankton – tiny plants and animals that float in the sea.

pollution – to harm our natural surroundings with chemicals and waste products.

produced water – water that is removed from newly drilled crude oil and then poured away into the sea.

regional sea – an enclosed or semi-enclosed sea.

solar power – energy from the Sun's rays.

toxic – poisonous.

INDEX

Photocredits

Abbreviations: l-left, r-right, b-bottom, t-top, c-centre, m-middle
Front cover l, 17b — Andrea Booher/ FEMA News Photo. Front cover r, back cover, 13t, 14bl, 21b, 27t — National Oceanic and Atmospheric Administration/Department of Commerce. 3— Robert Harding Photo Library. 4-5 — Photodisc. 6, 7 both, 8, 9, 12, 15b, 20bl, 22l, 23tr — Frank Spooner Pictures. 10l, 17t, 19br, 25b — Science Photo Library. 13b — RIA Novosti. 16, 18bl — Spectrum Colour Library. 24 — Select Pictures. 27t — TAPS. 27b — Corel.